M000074632

Faith, Family, and Fantasy

THE POETRY OF LINDA HUGHES

Linda Hughes

TRILOGY CHRISTIAN PUBLISHERS

Tustin, CA

Trilogy Christian Publishers

A Wholly Owned Subsidiary of Trinity Broadcasting Network

2442 Michelle Drive

Tustin, CA 92780

For information, address Trilogy Christian Publishing

Rights Department, 2442 Michelle Drive, Tustin, Ca 92780.

Trilogy Christian Publishing/ TBN and colophon are trademarks of Trinity Broadcasting Network.

For information about special discounts for bulk purchases, please contact Trilogy Christian Publishing.

Manufactured in the United States of America

Trilogy Disclaimer: The views and content expressed in this book are those of the author and may not necessarily reflect the views and doctrine of Trilogy Christian Publishing or the Trinity Broadcasting Network.

Cover image: Photo by Andrew Neel from Pexels

10 9 8 7 6 5 4 3 2 1

Library of Congress Cataloging-in-Publication Data is available.

ISBN 978-1-64088-531-8

ISBN 978-1-64088-532-5 (ebook)

Contents

A Mission at Christmastime

Emmanuel

Brownie Goes to Bethlehem

What Christmas Means to Me

Easter

The Warrior

Alone for Me

Midnight and Dawn

It Had to Be

Tell Me Again of Calvary

The Fountain

The Veil

Anniversary

To My Love

To Fall in Love

The Voyage

God Saw Us Through

My Sapphire Baby

The Old Preacher

My Husband—A Gift from God

The Journey

Two Feet

In His Presence

Childhood

It's Fall

Snow in Brownsville, Texas

Rainbows in My Sink

The Sunbeam

Vans

Central Supply

It Rhymes with "O"

The Halloween Party

Halloween Night

Halloween

The Witches' Cave

Me and Joshua

I'm Going Home

Because of My Sins

Bethesda's Pool

Let the Beauty of the Lord

This Same Jesus

This book is dedicated to all those wonderful people—family and friends—whose prayers, help, encouragement, and generosity have made it possible.

Thank you, and may God bless each one of you!

Acknowledgements

I would like to acknowledge Mr. Terry Cordingley, Ms. Christy Phillippe my project manager, and the staff at Trilogy Christian Publishing for their help, kindness, guidance, and patience in helping me through unchartered waters in making the dream of writing this book a reality.

Thank you from the bottom of my heart. May the richest of God's blessings be yours!

GUARDIAN OF THE RIVER

The water's deep; the waves are steep,
    But My grace will fail you never.
They'll not o'erflow as you onward go
    For I'm the Guardian of the river.

The river's wide at eventide,
    But fear no evil, ever.
I'll pilot thee o'er to that fair shore,
    For I'm the Guardian of the river.

When toiling's done, when day is gone,
    And Earth's lights for you quiver,
Tho the night is dark, I'll guide your barque,
    For I'm the Guardian of the river.

MY TOMORROWS

In all my tomorrows, I know He'll be there,
 Tho I'm burdened with sorrow and ladened with
  care.
Tho troubled and dreary my future may be,
 My soul, He will pilot, o'er life's stormy sea.

Anxiety doth ofttimes rule the heart;
 We wonder, will care ever from us depart?
As we look at tomorrow, our strength seems so frail,
 But He led through today; why should tomorrow He
  fail?

When I wake in the morning, He'll be waiting there,
 To lead through a day that may have its care.
Tho trouble and sorrow each new day may lend,
 Blessings, upon us, manifold, He doth send.

I leave all my future to One who doth know,
 The path that I follow; the way that I go.
His smile will bring sunshine; His joy will bring peace.
 In a golden tomorrow, my sorrow shall cease.

BUSINESS FOR THE KING

In humble hovels, homes so bare, oh, the needs that lin-
  ger there.
    The message of the Cross to bring: Urgent business
    for the King.

In mansions fair, that gleam so bright, souls in darkness of the night.
    To them, the story true must ring: Urgent business
    for the King.

On dusty roads, on highways grand, to and fro across
  the land.
    We toil and pray; we preach and sing: Urgent busi-
    ness for the King.

Work to be done, fields to glean—oh, the end so near
  is seen.
    Hurry, hurry, your sheaves to bring! Urgent busi-
    ness for the King.

The King's ambassadors are we, preaching Christ to
  bond and free.
    The world must hear with speed of wing: Urgent
    business for the King.

THE MAN AT THE CROSSROADS

Well, there I stood at the crossroads. Down a long,
    dusty road I had come.
    Two roads, only one I could follow, and I was weary
      and longing for home.
'Twas plain a choice I had to make, and none for me
    could choose.
    For if on the wrong road I did go, 'twas my own soul
      I would lose.

Many were taking the broad way; it's true, it seemed the
    best.
    But their furrowed brow and hurried pace, bespoke
      that they found no rest.
Seeking peace, I turned around the other way to see,
    And beheld, in the shadow of a cross, the Man of
      Galilee.

I knew Him at once; at His feet I bowed, and my hungry
    soul did cry.
    His gentle smile and compelling voice bade me this
      way to try.
I looked at the road. 'Twas very straight; the hills seemed
    to touch the sky,

With valleys so deep, shadows so dark, it seemed
fearsome to the eye.

His pleading voice I could not resist, as I heard Him
gently say,
"I'll hold your hand and commune with you as we
journey day by day."
"Look not to the right, nor to the left; see not the depth
nor height.
"Ye shall find peace, for there are pastures green,
and I shall be your light."

With His promise ringing in my ears, I gave my heart
to Him.
And tho many years we've walked this road, His
light has ne'er grown dim.
We've journeyed many a lonely mile; we've crossed the
hill and dale,
But never once has He left my side, nor has His
promise failed.

I find each day He's just the same as He was on that
first day,
When I met Him at the crossroads and did not
know the way.

GOD GIVETH PEACE

In a world of deep despair,
Beset by sin and bowed with care,
Turn to your God in humble prayer,
    God giveth peace.

When all around is black as night,
And nothing seems to turn out right,
When clouds blot out the morning light,
    God giveth peace.

Peace, while traveling down life's road;
Peace, while struggling with your load;
Peace, when entering death's abode;
    God giveth peace.

Peace I leave with you, my peace I give unto you; not as the world giveth, give I unto you. Let not your heart be troubled, neither let it be afraid.

                                —John 14:27

WHO WILL VOLUNTEER?

We are promised care and strife as foes, and many a
    bitter tear;
    A pathway filled with thorns and briars; who will
      volunteer?
Beset each day by trials anew, and on through passing
    years,
    For a battle that seems to never end, Jesus needs
      volunteers.

Amid the thorns are roses sweet, and Heaven's gates
    shine clear.
    Amid the battle is sweetest joy. Will you volunteer?
Many souls are lost and dying; their hungry hearts seek
    cheer.
    But I seem to hear you saying, "I dare not volunteer!"

"I cannot walk in thorny paths; mine eyes do loathe the
    tear.
    "A soft and easy road I seek' I cannot volunteer."
Still the battle goes on; o'er it all, the sweet voice of Je-
    sus I hear,
    Calling to all who walk life's road, "Will you
      volunteer?"

There are a few who dare to brave the task of the Master, dear.

Someday the Prince of Love will welcome home His volunteers.

BEGGAR

Beggar sat on the streets, in a crowd, yet alone,
 With a little tin cup and clothes that were torn.
People passed by and not one gave heed.
 They laughed at his plight and scoffed at his need.

Beggar had none of life's blessings to hold,
 And nobody wanted him, since he was old.
Comfortless, friendless, only God heard his cry.
 Sick in body and poor—how he wished he could die.

At its best, life's road for him had been steep;
 And one night he drifted into death's dreamless
  sleep.
Bright angels stood by to carry him o'er
 A deep-flowing river to the heavenly shore.

They dressed him in robes—long, radiant, and white—
 And neared jasper walls, resplendently bright.
Trumpeters sounded their notes loud and clear.
 A herald's voice called, "Thy son, Beggar, is here."

Through great pearly gates, to a city of gold,
 Beggar thought when he saw it, "The half was not
  told."

The great city echoed with the voice of a shout:
Hosannas were ringing; there was joy all about.

Palm leaves were waved, and golden crowns shone.
Saints by the millions had safely reached home.
He saw Father and Mother; they had been gone so long.
And o'er Heaven's skies rolled redemption's sweet song.

To the foot of the throne, lowly Beggar was led,
And the King of all kings placed a crown on his head.
While his tears flowed, the Savior said, "Welcome home, son.
"Thy anguish and toiling and sighing is done.

"Here, thou art not a beggar, nor hungry or cold,
"But thou art My son and one of My fold.
"Thou shalt live here with Me, through eternity's day.
"Thy pilgrimage has ended; thou art home to stay."

Humble Beggar was given a mansion so fair.
He was laden with gifts and treasures quite rare.
Far o'er Heaven's scene, only beauty to see.
In peaceful habitations, forever to be.

The Spider and the Palace

Once on a far-off, distant strand
    'Midst a green and fertile land,
There was a palace with marble walls,
    Stately turrets, and gilded halls.

The palace sat, bedecked and fair,
    With battlements manned and treasures rare.
Its unfurled banners proudly waved,
    And many a battle it fiercely braved.

One day, while the Keeper was unaware,
    A Spider crept in that palace fair.
He found a corner and went to work,
    And from his task, he did not shirk.

Although his presence now is known,
    Because his web has larger grown,
He toils and spins without reproof,
    From cellar low, to highest roof.

Tiny silvery, silken strands,
    They're strong as any metal band.
Twining 'round each spot they meet,
    And blocking Heaven's light, so sweet.

You can't get through the Palace hall;
　　The dirty webs hang over all.
The Keeper has long been fast asleep;
　　Darkness and dust o'er all do creep.

The fertile valley still is green;
　　The marble walls still have their sheen;
Outside its beauty all can see,
　　While inside, the spider works with glee.

Lord, set watchmen by our lips
　　To help us weigh each word that slips,
That no evil spider may come in;
　　That You would find us free from sin.

The spider taketh hold with her hands, and is in kings' palaces.
　　　　　　　　　　　　　　　—Proverbs 30:28

THE MERCY SEAT

Kings in gold apparel,
Beggars with unshod feet,
Have knelt in deep contrition
Here at the Mercy Seat.

A fountain, deep, is flowing;
Christ's presence is so sweet.
If thou would truly be made clean,
Bow at the Mercy Seat.

Balm for every heartache;
Victory for defeat;
Joy for deepest sorrow;
Is at the Mercy Seat.

Tearstains on the altar
Where God and man do meet.
There's room for one more burden
Down at the Mercy Seat.

THE HEAT OF THE BATTLE

In the heat of the battle, oh, Soul, so oppressed.
The tempest is raging while Powers do wrest.
In the heat of the battle, with night coming on,
The victory looks farther away than at dawn.

The blood of brave men lies spilt on the ground;
The cry of the wounded is heard all around.
To the heat of the battle, Christ's banners still lead.
We dare not look back; souls still are in need.

Through Christ we shall conquer, tho all Hell surrounds.
In the heat of the battle, Lord, may I be found!

BARTIMAEUS

Bartimaeus! Bartimaeus! Clad in rags and blind in eye.
  Bartimaeus, son of Timaeus, Jesus of Nazareth
    passeth by!

Bartimaeus, don't just sit there! He hath heard thy des-
    perate plea!
  Cast away thy beggar's garments! Rise, for He hath
    called for thee!

Bartimaeus, hear the Savior, with deepest love and
    mercy, say,
  "Bartimaeus, what wilt thou have Me to do for thee
    today?"

Bartimaeus, tell Him plainly all the longing of thy soul!
  He will touch thee, gently touch thee, and thy blind
    eyes shall be whole.

Bartimaeus, leap rejoicing! Raise thy voice above earth's
    din!
  "He has healed me! He has healed me!" Bartimaeus
    sees again!

HERE COMES JESUS

My ship was being battered by angry, pounding waves.
Dark, threatening clouds above me, I cried, "Oh, can
none save?"
And here comes Jesus!

He spoke, and all the pounding of angry waves did
cease,
The sun peeped through the clouds, as o'er the stormy
seas,
Here comes Jesus.

The road was long and winding; I faltered on the way.
My hungry, thirsting soul cried, "Save, oh, save, I pray!"
And here comes Jesus!

He spoke, and with the manna from Heaven, I was
filled.
His joy, He put within me, and song within me thrilled.
Here comes Jesus.

Temptations; raging sicknesses—I felt my spirit quiver.
Too many problems in my life, I cried, "Can none
deliver?"
And here comes Jesus!

He spoke, and burdens lifted; my body was made whole.
He told me that He loved me and saved my wandering
 soul.
 Here comes Jesus.

The world is rocking, reeling; no peace can now be
 found.
In the midst of all the problems, I hear the trumpet
 sound!
 And here comes Jesus!

In the twinkling of an eye, we're caught away, caught
 away!
All the problems left behind; we've all gone home to
 stay!
 Here comes Jesus!

LORD, I WOULD WALK WITH THEE

Through barren, steaming deserts, or pastures, lush
    and green;
When light is falling on my path, or when no way can
    be seen;
    Lord, I would walk with Thee.

While stumbling up the mountainside or shouting
    from its peak;
When long have been the nighttime hours and the sun's
    warm glow I seek;
    Lord, I would walk with Thee.

Upon the rough and rock-strewn path, tho slow my
    steps may be,
I would follow all the way the bleeding prints of Calvary.
    Lord, I would walk with Thee.

Through all my days, until life's end and the crossing
    looms in view,
When the muddy Jordan is at hand and I must pass on
    through,
    Lord, I would walk with Thee.

AUDIENCE WITH THE KING

The door to the throne room is open,
My Father, the King, there abides.
I hear His voice gently calling my name,
Bidding me just step inside.

His scepter is held out toward me,
He never has turned me away.
His smile makes me know I am welcome;
He lovingly bids me to stay.

Precious to me are the moments spent
In audience with the King.
He patiently listens while I tell Him all,
My burdens; my joys; everything!

When the day's been long and weary,
Just to sit down at His feet
Brings a quiet rest upon my soul.
He can make the bitter sweet.

When blessings come, when joys abound,
When faith is riding high,
This, too, I want to share with Him,
So, I hasten to His side.

I'd love to stay in this hallowed place,
And commune with Him always.
But I must go and do the work
He bids me do today.

Yes, I treasure golden moments
When, in answer to my ring,
The door to the Throne Room opens,
And I am in audience with the King.

THE CANDLE OF THE LORD

I asked the Lord to search my heart, for I would enter in
That blissful home for all His saints, and there could be
no sin.
Now, He would have no problems for I kept my house
clean!
Had I not served Him all my days? His fields, I'd tried
to glean.

So, the Lord, His candle lit, He came to my heart's door.
I eagerly bade Him to come in and search through my
heart's store.
Through all the chambers of my heart, every corner, every room.
The candle of the Lord burned bright; each spot it did
illume.

His eyes, filled with love and pity, tenderly looked at
me.
He said, "Do you see as I do?" I wept as I sank to my
knees.
My righteousness, as filthy rags, lay scattered on the
floor.
Forgotten webs hung from the walls; clutter was door
to door.

The windows were smudged and dirty; no light went in
or out.
Messy corners were filled with trash I'd just forgotten
about.
I cried, "Oh, God, I did not know! I've been too blind to
see.
"I promise You, Lord, I'll clean it up!" Then He spoke
lovingly.

"Dear child, that's been the problem now; by yourself,
it's been in vain.
"If you will trust My cleansing power, you can be clean
again."
"Oh, yes, dear Lord," I humbly cried. "Please make me
white as snow.
"Wash me again in Calvary's tide, that crimson, cleansing flow."

In deep contrition at His feet, I felt His Spirit touch me.
I was renewed and sanctified! I sang the song of vict'ry!
I looked around at what had been so dirty and unclean,
And now, behold, all things were new, sparkling, bright,
and clean!

The cluttered mess was gone, and through the windows
came the light!

The Prince of Peace was in my heart! All things were
   pure and bright!
I thank God for His candle, His Word that pierces
   through
All sham and pretense, fear and doubt, and keeps our
   path in view.

And so, I daily read His Word and praise Him for the
   knowing.
He cleansed my heart. Oh, happy day! To Heaven, I am
   going!

CHURCH WITHOUT GOD

Church without God! Our eyebrows raise in righteous
    indignation!
And yet each day, more churches slip into this satanic,
    unholy situation.
It doesn't happen all at once. It's so gradual no one sees.
A church that once was full of power is no longer on its
    knees.

They sit so proudly in the pews, sung to by a silk-robed
    choir.
The plate is passed; a prayer is said; and they carefully
    watch the hour.
The minister stands behind his desk; no emotion at all
    is shown.
A benediction is solemnly said; it's all over, so they go
    home.

What happened to the churches? What happened to the
    power?
What happened to those holy people that walked with
    God each hour?
They used to shout and weep and cry and spend their
    nights in prayer.

Sinners saved, and lives were changed. The town knew
the church was there!

But now, we don't need emotion. We're taught that's all
"passe."
"Just believe you're right with God and go on your mer-
ry way!"
"We must control the service now. Don't preach too
hard on sin!"
They're passing regulations that God's laws never entered in.

They say the Bible is outdated; it doesn't work for us
today.
They don't believe in Heaven or Hell, so why walk a holy
way?
They can't give God the authority to perform a virgin
birth;
So, Jesus was not the Son of God; just another good
Man on earth.

They sent God away from the door of their church, His
Spirit welcomed no more.
And so, with bazaars and social encounters they strive
for the heavenly shore.

Church without God? Yes, church without God, it's
    clear.
No sinners are saved; no lives are changed; and the
    town never knows they are there.

JESUS DREW NEAR

My load of sin was heavy; my heart was plagued with
   fear.
My troubled soul sought comfort; then Jesus Himself
   drew near.
He called me from my weary way and gave me perfect
   rest.
I cast my load upon Him and knew His way was best.

As the shrouded gloomy specter of death was hovering
   near,
'Mid stinging tears of sorrow, Jesus Himself drew near.
The precious Balm of Gilead was poured upon my soul.
Through tears, I saw the sun shine; the wounded was
   made whole.

Through life's troubled, stormy seas, through paths of
   doubt and fear,
We find comfort, peace, and joy when Jesus Himself
   draws near.

THE CITY OF THE KING

Lord, set my face like a flint toward Zion, the City of the
      King.
Where white-robed saints, with golden crowns, their
      songs of triumph sing.

With jasper walls and golden streets, foundations rich
      and rare,
Where all is peace and none e'er cry, majestic home so
      fair.

I have determined to enter there, tho fierce the fight
      may be.
Bought by the blood of the dying Lamb, who gave Him-
      self for me.

The enemy surrounds us as we go; many battles there
      may be.
But when the smoke has cleared away, my home I want
      to see.

Still on my way and straight on course, tho battle-
      scarred, I sing.
Lord, set my face like a flint toward Zion, the City of the
King.

For the LORD God will help me; therefore shall I not be con-founded: therefore have I set my face like a flint, and I know that I shall not be ashamed.

—Isaiah 50:7

I SAW YOU THERE

When your head was bowed with sorrow,
And your shoulders slumped with care,
When with pain, you saw tomorrow,
I saw you standing there.

When your tears fell down unbidden,
And your soul filled with despair,
All alone, from man's eye hidden,
I saw you weeping there.

When you wandered in dry places,
Through valleys dark and drear,
When your strength gave in the races,
I saw you walking there.

I girded you with my great love;
I bottled all your tears.
Mine eye did guide you from above.
Child, I was with you there.

THE WATCHMAN

Watchman! Watchman, upon the wall,
Midnight draweth nigh!
Have you the trumpet ready in hand
To sound the battle cry?

Are your eyes alert for the gathering hordes
That prepare to storm the wall?
Have you warned the people to be armed
That the City might not fall?

Have you yet caught sight of the enemy's camp?
Have you seen their banners fly?
Do you see their spears and habergeons
Glint in the darkened sky?

The King hath set thee on the wall.
Oh, do not fall asleep!
He has placed the City in your hands;
You have a charge to keep.

Upon your hands, the King hath said
The stains of blood will be.
If the people are slain at the enemy's hand
And are not warned to flee.

What will you say when the King returns
And sees the City's plight?
What will you answer when He says to you,
"Watchman, Watchman, what of the night?"

THE GOLD IS IN THE FIRE

A shattered dream, a promise broken, a loss of heart's
    desire,
Days of grief and nights of sorrow—the gold is in the
    fire.

An unkind word that cut and stung; someone raised
    your ire!
A trusted friend became your foe—the gold is in the
    fire.

A sickness with no cure at hand; a future, bleak and
    dire;
A sudden death of someone dear—the gold is in the fire.

When neither God nor man will hear and help you
    through the mire,
It seems you walk the way alone—the gold is in the fire.

Being cleansed and purified, a vessel, lifted higher,
So a holy God can dwell within—the gold is in the fire.

THE REVIEW

The Lord came down to review His troops, as any good
    general would.
He stepped into the reviewing stand, and Satan, beside
    Him, stood.
He looked at God with an impudent face, and said with
    an insolent smirk,
"Why do You bother Yourself with this? You know if
    men do Your work."

God gave him a look that said, "Be quiet"; and so, the
    review began.
With their colors streaming, many souls marched past
    the reviewing stand.
The first of these were polished and shined, decked out
    with degrees and bars.
Satan said, "Well, here now, I'm impressed..." But God
    said, "I see no scars."

"I do not understand You!" Satan said, with his nose
    way out of joint.
"Now, all of these look fine to me!" And God said, "That's
    My point!"
The next in line were a noisy bunch, all dressed for a
    day at the beach.

Satan yelled out, "IT'S PARTY TIME," and stepped back
    out of God's reach.

"But they look happy," Satan sulked. "You don't let peo-
    ple play."
"It appears to Me," God sadly said, "they'd be better off
    to pray."
Those who came next were most unkempt, with bleary
    eyes and cough.
A bottle was passed from hand to hand, their cadence
    clearly off.

"Hmm," said Satan. "These tarried too long at Your
    communion cup.
"How nice of You to provide for them." And God said,
    "Satan, shut up!"
And then the final wave came into view; their robes
    were a glorious white.
The battle scars were plain to see, hard won from many
    a fight.

Their march was perfect symmetry; their armor, bright
    and strong.
Two-edged swords were in their hands; "Hallelujah"
    was their song.

"Well now," said God, with a look of pride, "would you take a look at these!

"It does appear that they survived when you knocked them to their knees!"

"What is this bunch doing here? I had them counted out!

"How do they keep coming back?" Satan yelled out with a shout.

"Thought you had them, huh." God laughed. "I'd say this review is through.

"The last of these are clearly Mine; the rest belong to you!"

BELIEVE IN ME

It matters not in God's great plan if Jairus's child lies
    sleeping,
And all her family and friends are gathered 'round her
    weeping.
It matters not that Jairus is told, "Trouble Him no
    more."
For she has passed the portal of death and is on the oth-
    er shore.

But feel his pain and see his grief, for Jesus has tarried
    long.
Too many people thronging Him, and now his child is
    gone.
Then Jesus turns to him and speaks. "Fear not; she's just
    asleep.
"I say to you, believe in Me, and do not grieve nor weep."

It's hard to stand aside and wait until the Master comes.
Harder still to just believe when hope seems lost and
    gone.
He stares into her vacant face and feels his heart will
    break.
Even though Jesus is now here, can He his child awake?

Jesus reaches and takes her hand; He speaks with love
and grace.
"Young maid, I say to thee, arise." And light comes to
her face.
Jairus's heart with wonder thrills, and tears of joy run
free!
The Giver of Life has entered the room, and death has
had to flee!

So, if you walk with shattered dreams, and life seems
all in vain;
Your heart bleeds, and bitter tears fall to the ground
like rain;
Hear Jesus say, "Believe in Me. Do not doubt nor fear."
And though He tarries, wait for Him; your heart He'll
fill with cheer.

It matters not what barriers stand, for they are swept
away.
For He brings life and joy and peace when He comes in
to stay.

FINDING GOLD

I lived in a town called "Sin-Holds-Sway" on the banks
of a murky stream.
Seeking life's fortune and finding none, I chased the
elusive dream.
On the dirty streets of this filthy town was sold the souls
of men
Who came for gold, but found, at last, the empty life of
sin.

I panned the stream in search of gold, but pyrite filled
my pans.
And though I wasted many years, no gold came to my
hands.
There were days of sighing, nights of pain; I wished for
a better way.
For life was passing swiftly by; my debts, I could not
pay.

One day while panning in the stream, on the other
shore there stood
A Man who said, "Come; follow Me to a place where the
gold is good."
I yearned to leave this filthy place but could not cross
the tide,

For it was full of trash and mud; no bridge to the other
    side.

He said, "I have made a way for you." And across the
    stream there fell
A bloodstained tree shaped like a cross; faint hope be-
    gan to swell.
Was this for real? How could it be? Thinking it must be
    a dream,
Trembling with fear, yet eager to go, I crossed o'er the
    murky stream.

The love in His eyes said it was real! He held me with
    tender embrace
In spite of my rags, all covered with mire; I marveled at
    such loving grace.
He silenced my questions with, "Follow Me. All of your
    debts I have paid."

I couldn't hold back the hot, stinging tears, when I
    learned of the sacrifice made.

My vile rags were traded for a robe so clean; my soul, He
    washed with His blood.
I knelt at His feet and knew I would follow Him, even
    through fire and flood.

He gently led me with His hand to a place so bright and
    fair.
No dirty streets; no filthy streams; no sin could enter
    there.

All is at peace within my heart as I daily pan the stream,
Wade out into its flowing waters, and gather the gold
    of my dreams.
This river Pison flows all around the land of Havilah's
    wood.
There is bdellium and the onyx stone, and the gold of
    that land is good.

And a river went out of Eden to water the garden; and from
thence it was parted, and became into four heads. The name of
the first is Pison: that is it which compasseth the whole land of
Havilah, where there is gold; and the gold of that land is good:
there is bdellium and the onyx stone.

—Genesis 2:10–12

I STILL BELIEVE

I still believe that Jesus Christ was born in Bethlehem
Of a virgin mother and laid to sleep in a rough, crude
feeding bin.
I still believe that shepherds ran to see the infant King,
When Heaven's hosts in darkened skies made "Hallelu-
jahs" ring!
I still believe that Eastern kings paid visit from afar;
Presenting gifts to honor Him, led by that glorious star!

I still believe He walked the shores of Galilee's blue sea.
He healed the sick and raised the dead; dumb spoke
and blind could see.
I still believe that by His death, I am from sin set free;
His precious blood that fell that day flows down to cov-
er me.
I still believe that He arose and came out from the tomb;
Conquering death, hell, and the grave, enlightening the
gloom.

I still believe that He ascended in clouds to Heaven
above,
And is seated now at God's right hand, where He pleads
for me in love.
I still believe He'll come for me to take me to that shore

Of Heaven, golden city fair, to stay forevermore.

Ofttimes the doubts and fears arise, and dark clouds
threaten me.

It's then Faith whispers in my heart, "I still believe! I
still believe!"

IN SEARCH OF ONE

I opened the door at the dawn of creation;
God's glory met me there.
I gazed in awe at its pristine beauty;
His light shone everywhere!
I walked with Him through Eden's Garden
And saw man's dreadful fall;
I trembled in terror as the sentence was read
And death pronounced upon all.
Yet in love and mercy, I heard Him tell
Of the One who would one day come
To destroy the power of deceiver and death
And restore fallen man to his home.

With hearts full of grief, we left Eden behind
To enter a world filled with pain.
Then down through the corridors of time,
We searched for that One in vain.
Many prophets and kings heard the promise renewed,
To send the Deliverer to them;
Yet though they believed and waited and prayed,
Not one had proved to be Him.
Many hundreds of years had now come and gone,
Then one day near deep Jordan's wood,
Where John was baptizing all those who would come,

In the midst of the crowd, there He stood!

As He stepped from the water, I knew it was Him.
God spoke so vibrant and clear!
"This is My Son. With Him I am pleased!"
The heavenly Dove hovered near.
He left Jordan in the power of God's might;
The One, long sought, had arrived!
But because He spoke of love and not war,
The Lamb was crucified.
I heard the voice of the great God say,
 "It is done; the debt is now paid.
"Fallen man can now return to his home.
"By Jesus, the way has been made!"

For by His precious, spilled-out blood,
For all time, death and sin
Have been destroyed, and the gates of Eden
Are now opened once again.
I opened the door at the close of Creation
And gazed in awe once more.
The light of God will forever shine
On the heavenly Eden's shore.

THEY SAY

They say You ain't a'coming, Lord, that You've done
    closed up shop!
And You don't answer no more prayers, though we pray
    until we drop!
They say there's no such thing as sin; anything goes, it
    seems.
The devil's just an old wives' tale to haunt the children's
    dreams.

They're not real sure that You exist; Your law sits on a
    shelf.
Each one of us is a little god—just find your inner self!
Well, that might be okay for some, but I think I'll take
    Your way.
'Cause I still think Your shop is open and You answer
    when I pray!

Imagine! Conjuring up this stuff and wasting perfect
    minds!
What must You think when they ignore the truths they
    all could find?
And I wonder what they'll say, Lord, when, contrary to
    their view,

You return and they find out that what You said was
   true!

THOUGHTS OF HOME

When You walked along earth's pathways, did You stop
and smell the flowers?
Did the roses and the lilies make You think of Heaven's
bowers?
After stormy rains and thunder, when the rainbow
brightly shone
Across the sky with splashing colors, did it make You
think of Home?

Traveling down the many roadways, thick dust clinging
to Your feet,
Did You remember, with the angels, walking Heaven's
golden street?
When You visited with many folks in homes of every
kind,
Were ivory palaces of Heaven ever pictured in Your
mind?

When You felt the gentle comfort of a dear friend's
warm embrace,
Did it fill You with a longing just to see the Father's face?
You left behind so very much; I'll never know, You see,
How You could leave that Glory-land for just the love
of me!

COMMISSIONED

"Commissioned! ME, LORD??? You want me to go
WHERE????
"Why, I don't know those people, Lord! I can't go over
THERE!!!!!"

"Well, yes, I have commissioned you—see Matthew
twenty-eight.
"And if you don't go, child, then for them, it may well be
too late."

"Now, Lord, You know I'm slow of speech and as bash-
ful as can be.
"I know I must have heard wrong, Lord; You surely
don't mean ME!!!"

"Well, yes, I really did mean YOU! And let Me remind
you here,
"When Moses used this same excuse, I helped him with
his fear."

"Well, Lord, You have to understand, my schedule's full
right now.
"I'd love to accommodate You, Lord, but I really don't
see how!"

"Yes, speaking of busy schedules, want to trade yours
for Mine?

"Go get folks ready for eternity, their souls all on the
line."

"Keeping in mind that I have to work with folks who
won't obey,

"My pleas often fall on stopped-up ears, but there is no
other way.

"I left Heaven to accommodate you on Calvary's bloody
brow.

"So, yes, I have commissioned you, and child, the time
is NOW!!!

"I said I'd go all the way with you; I've provided all you
need.

"All of Heaven stands with you with full authority.

"I need someone to tell the world salvation's full and
free.

"I have commissioned you to go. Will you not go for
Me?"

THE PATHS

I thank You for paths in stormy seas
When floods come in to threaten me.
When lightning flashes and sunlight flees,
    You walk with me.

I thank You for the paths of night
When all seems lost and hope takes flight;
Your written Word my only light;
    You walk with me.

I thank You for the paths of fire
When ease of pain is my desire;
Because the flames lick ever higher;
    You walk with me.

I thank You for the paths serene,
For flowering shrubs so lush and green;
Guided by Your hand, unseen,
    You walk with me.

No matter where the path may lead,
Through brightest joy or darkest deed,
Your hand supplies my every need;
    You walk with me.

YOU ARE THAT GOD

You are that God of Noah's flood, of the rainbow in the
    sky.
That God of Abraham's sacrifice, when the ram, not
    Isaac, died.
You are that God of the Exodus, of the pillars of cloud
    and fire;
That God of Jericho's crumbling walls, and of Hannah's
    heart's desire.
You are that God of Elijah's prayers, when the fire from
    Heaven came;
That God of Daniel's lions' den, when he called upon
    Your name.

You are that God when the widow of Nain received her
    son alive;
That healed the sick and calmed the seas; of Bethesda's
    porches, five.
You are that God of Pentecost, with the cloven tongues
    and wind;
That God of Paul's Damascus Road; You brought the
    Gentiles in.
What You did for those people of old, we need You to
    do today!

Please rend the heavens and come down; come, visit us,
    we pray.

We stand in need of You, dear God; our times are bleak
    and dire!
We repent of our sins, our failures, God; please light
    our altar fires!
We need another Pentecost, a parting of the seas!
We need these walls to crumble down, the lions' mouths
    to cease!
Revive, renew, and raise us up! Give a new Damascus
    Road,
That we may go and compel them in to Your eternal
    fold!

ONE VOICE

I listened in awe as voices raised in glorious harmony,
To sing the praises of our God, with spirits full and free.
And then I heard as one lone voice arose above the
crowd;
Out of sync and a bit off-key, and, with gusto, sang
aloud!

Although it did distract a bit, and the leader really tried,
He was oblivious to them all! For him, the Lord had
died!
His eyes were closed, his hands upraised; he was lost to
all around!
And though some people looked annoyed, it was a joyous sound!

I know that Heaven listened in to hear this one lone
voice.
By worldly standards frowned upon; unto His Lord,
rejoice!
When Heaven's choir has gathered home and singing
fills the air,
I know that somewhere in that crowd, in a place of hon-
or there,

Will be the man who loved his Lord. And do you know
    what I think?
Jesus won't mind if he is singing off-key and out of
    sync!

DID I MAKE JESUS SMILE?

The traffic was outrageous, folks darting in and out!
Honking loudly, gesturing—it's enough to make one
shout.

Was I a party to their madness? Was I all that I could
be?
In my reactions to their raging, did I make Jesus smile
at me?

Someone really punched my buttons—hateful, caustic,
lying words;
Tempers flaring; voices raising; vicious rumors
overheard.

Did I let God control my spirit till the dust had settled
down?
Or did I explode in anger? Did I make Jesus smile or
frown?

In any given situation when it seems that Hell holds
sway,
Did I draw strength from Living Waters? Did I make
Jesus smile today?

I'M THANKFUL

I'm thankful for salvation free, and for the Christ, who
  died for me.
I'm thankful for the life He gives, and that I am allowed
  to live.
I'm thankful for each breath I take, and for each dawn
  that I awake.
I'm thankful for the health He brings, for music that
  gives my heart its wings.

I'm thankful for life's sunny days and stormy clouds, so
  dark and gray.
I'm glad I hear the birds that sing and for yellow roses
  in the spring.
I'm thankful for my family tree, for all the ones so dear
  to me:
My children, plus the grand- and great-, their smiles
  are lights within my gates.

I'm thankful for the home He gave, for roof and walls,
  and special days.
I'm thankful for all things within, and for the special
  gift of friends.
I'm thankful for the life I've had, for all the times, both
  good and bad.

I've learned to lean on His strong arm and know that I
am safe from harm.

And if I've forgotten any part, may the great God, who
knows the heart,
Search all the corners there and find a thankful heart
and a grateful mind.

DINING WITH GOD

I love to dine at Your table!
I draw from the strength You provide:
To converse in holy communion,
Sitting in peace by Your side.

The time just goes by so swiftly,
It seems we've hardly begun.
The sweetness of joy in Your presence
Outshines the clear morning sun!

Ofttimes I come wearied and troubled
And, as always, You know what I need.
I begin to dig into Your bounty
You've placed, lovingly, there for me.

The dishes are always filled to the brim;
My heart, with Your joy, overflows.
I drink Living Waters and Milk of the Word
And commune with Sharon's sweet Rose.

I return to Your table time and again;
The blest Bread of Life is my stay.
I joyously dine, rejoice, and partake
Of Your table, my strength for my days.

A WINTER'S DAY

Often when the morning dawns, the sky is dark and
 gray.
The wind is blowing, bitter cold; it's a typical Winter's
 Day.
I shiver some and turn away from the window with a
 sigh
And wonder what I'll do today, since it seems I'm stuck
 inside.

Then a soft and gentle whisper resounds within my ear,
"Come and spend the day with Me! There are things
 that you should hear."
He takes me lovingly through His Word, and it seems
 each verse I read
Shows how with tender mercy, His people He would
 lead:
Often through deep, troubled waters, and often through
 the fire,
But always His hand was open to give their hearts'
 desire.

So, if you're feeling housebound on a cold and blustery
 day,

Just spend some time with Jesus. It will chase the
    "blahs" away!
You will realize you have no reason for your world to be
    so dim.
Just listen to His gentle voice and spend some time
    with Him.

SOUNDS OF HEAVEN

Yes, I know within all reason that I'm still on this side.
And in my human form have not crossed o'er that Great
    Divide.
Yet there are times when in my soul it seems I've left
    this shore
And stand rejoicing as I hear the sounds at Heaven's
    Door.

Oft' when I hear the laughter of little ones at play,
The lilting, sweet, melodious sounds can catch my soul
    away.
I feel I'm standing at the door of Heaven and I hear
The sweetest laughter, joy, and praise ring out and fill
    my ear!

I listen as the saints of God rejoice with voices raised
Unto their God, who reigns above, and sing aloud His
    praise.
It seems I can hear the angels strike up their harps of
    gold;
Then my weary soul takes wing and listens at Heaven's
    Door.

There are so many cloud-filled days; sometimes the
      path is drear.
And then I hear a sound from Heaven, and it fills my
      heart with cheer.
The joyous laughter and glorious song can lift me up
      once more.
Until it seems that once again, I'm listening at Heaven's
      Door.

THE TRAVELERS

The way grew weary for those lonely three;
Joseph and Mary and the little donkey.
Uphill and downhill and, yes, all around,
Wending their way to Bethlehem-Town.
Caesar'd declared, "The world shall be taxed!"
The world didn't agree, but then, he hadn't asked.

Soon the lights of the little city appear;
The end of their journey was then very near.
Eager for rest, Joseph knocked on a door;
"No room in here," the innkeeper roared!
"No room in the inn! Now what shall we do?"
Joseph and Mary searched the whole city through.

The Travelers were not very costly arrayed,
And people gave it no thought when they turned them
        away.
But no place could be found for their weary heads,
Except for a stable, where cattle were fed.
And there in that barn, right in back of the inn,
Was born our King Jesus, the Savior of men.

Mary wrapped Him so tenderly. "Where shall He lay?"
"Oh, yes, the manger, full of sweet-smelling hay."

The animals gathered; they were first to behold
The sight that the Prophets of old had foretold.
"A beautiful Babe!" they all quickly agreed.
They didn't care that He lay on their feed.

While out on the hillside, the shepherds all throng;
Angels have appeared and are singing a song.
Sheep are forgotten, as they stand and hear,
The angels' message of hope and good cheer.
"A Savior! A Savior! Oh, praise His dear name!"
Some shout and some cry, feeling no shame.

"Oh, come, let us hasten to Bethlehem now,
"And worship the King, and at His feet bow!"
They enter the stable, and the feeling's so strong
That God and His Heaven are around looking on—
An awesome feeling for so humble a place.
Ah, but there in the manger, lies a Child full of grace.

"A beautiful Babe!" The Animals looked at each other.
"That's just what we said, each one to another!"
The shepherds went down, some on knees that were old
To worship the Child, of whom the angels had told.
The Wise Men came with their gifts, from afar,
Led by the light of a beautiful Star.

Just a couple of travelers in Bethlehem that night;
From each door turned away—what a pitiful sight.
But that night God's glory was made manifest,
And from that humble stable came a Child who was
      blest.
His destiny was to be hanged on a tree,
And be the great Sacrifice for you and for me.

MR. ROBIN'S RED BREAST

T'was a beautiful night on Bethlehem's plain.
The moon shone in splendor on rock and on grain.
The stars were shining, as if to say,
"God loves the world in a special way."
'Neath Mr. Robin's nest of twigs
Shepherds were munching their grapes and figs.
He heard them speak of many things,
As he, very quietly, folded his wings.

The sheep were sleeping; the fire was aglow;
All was peaceful there below.
Mr. Robin sighed and was closing his eyes
When loud singing voices filled the skies!
Mr. Robin nearly fell out of his nest!
The idea of someone disturbing his rest!
The sky seemed afire with a heavenly light.
The shepherds were trembling with awesome fright.

Many angels were singing, with voices clear.
Mr. Robin pricked up his ears to hear.
They told of a Child, God's Son, to be sure;
Born that night of a virgin, pure.
And if they would go to Bethlehem-Town.
They would find Him wrapped in swaddling-gown.

Lying in a manger, on the hay,
And singing, "Praise to God," the angels vanished away.

Well, Mr. Robin was all a'twitter!
The thrill in his heart had made his eyes glitter!
"I must go see," he said to his mate.
"Now, don't wait up, for I may be late."
So, off he flew, with speed of wing,
To see the Child, the Infant King.
For within his tiny heart, he knew
That this must be the Messiah, true.

He flew into the stable, that humble place,
And sat where he could see the Baby's face.
T'was sweet and gentle, pure and kind;
No fault, at all, in the Babe, did he find.
His heart filled with peace as he gazed upon
The face of his Creator's beloved Son.
His whole being swelled with melody, sweet,
As he flew to pay homage at His feet.

But what was this? There came thru the dark,
From the flame of fire, a living spark.
Mr. Robin grew worried and then he fled,
To stand between the fire and bed.
In the gap he stood till the night was o'er;

His feathers would be the same no more.
His breast had caught the sparks, so dire,
Now, a bright orange-red it was from the fire.

Mr. Robin hadn't uttered a single sound.
But then, the mother turned around.
She knew at once what he had done;
Endangered his life for her newborn Son.
She smiled at him and then replied,
"Tonight, you surely might have died.
"So great a love as you have shown
"Shall unto all men, be made known."

And when Mr. Robin's sons were born
He was reminded of her words that morn,
For upon their breasts, like a tiny pyre,
Danced the bright red-orange of the Vigil Fire.

GOD'S TREASURE

Joy-bells were ringing in Heaven;
Gladness was heard without measure.
    In the midst of Earth's night,
     God looked on its plight,
And gave unto men His Treasure.

Long bound by laws and tradition,
Sinking still deeper in sin,
    When in His great love,
     God sent from above,
His Treasure to dwell among men.

Straight from the ivory towers,
To a manger-bed filled with hay,
    The Fairest of Heaven;
     To man, freely given.
To redeem us, God made a way.

LITTLE TREE

Little Tree, festooned so bright,
Were you there that Holy Night?
When the Christ-Child came to earth,
Were you a witness at His birth?

When the heavens with carols rang,
Did you hear the angels sing?
When the Magi came from far,
Did you see that glorious Star?

Oh, I know you're just a tree,
Dressed up for all the kids to see.
But somehow when I look at you
The glory of that night shines through.

I sense the wonder the shepherds felt
As down on bended knee they knelt.
I seem to see the Eastern Kings,
Their precious gifts of homage bring.

I feel the joy of Christmas Day,
As 'round your green skirt, children play.
And I know for sure, that now, as then,
God's Gift was given to all men.

THE MESSIAH IS BORN

But the king didn't know!
Who'd tell the king of such a thing,
That o'er the hills the angels sang?

The queen didn't know.
Bathed in milk and robed in silk,
The poor, she only used to bilk.

The innkeeper didn't know.
Though they could pay, they were turned away
By his, "No room in here to stay!"

But the Wise Men knew.
A watchful eye against the sky,
Led by a Star to the Baby's side.

The shepherds knew.
They heard the song from Heaven's throng,
For they had waited patient, long.

And I know.
That glorious night, so radiant, bright,
Has illumed my heart with Heaven's light.

I'M SO GLAD HE CAME

A young man asked a question of me.
He was quite sincere, I must say.
Did I believe December the twenty-fifth
Was really the Lord's birthday?

I replied that no one knew for sure
What month or day to proclaim.
But why did it matter, for He was born,
And I am so glad He came.

I'm glad for the story of Joseph and Mary,
To God, submitting their wills.
For their long journey to far Bethlehem,
Nestled in the Judean hills.

For the inn; the innkeeper; the old stable-barn;
The manger-bed, all filled with hay.
Where, wrapped in those tiny swaddling-clothes,
The blessed Christ-Child lay.

For the shepherds, who watched over all their flock,
And trembled with such awesome fright.
When angels appeared and their glorious song
Rang out into Bethlehem's night.

I'm glad for the Star and the kings of the East,
Who opened their treasure to bring:
The gold and the myrrh and the sweet frankincense
To honor the new Infant King.

I'm glad they called His name Jesus;
His people from sin, He would save.
This sleepy Babe, soothed by Mary's soft song
Would break sin's hold o'er the slave.

I'm glad I know this story is true,
That God, in His great love for man,
Allowed His own Son to become "One of us"
And so bring Redemption's great plan.

So, no matter the month, the day, or the year,
The story is ever the same.
God gave the Best that He had to the world.
And I am so glad He came!

A MISSION AT CHRISTMASTIME

An angel came to the gate of Heaven looking haggard
    and forlorn.
His halo awry, his wings askew, his robe was dirty and
    torn.
"Heavenly days!" the gatekeeper cried, as he helped him
    to a chair.
"I thought your mission was one of peace! What hap-
    pened to you down there?"

The angel sighed and shook his head. "Yes, it was sup-
    posed to be.
"But it's hard to herald Christmas joy when fighting is
    all you see.
"I was narrowly missed by a hand grenade when I said,
    'I come in peace';
"I was caught between their mortar fire when I said,
    'Let all strife cease'!

"I barely escaped an angry mob when I mentioned
    brotherhood.
"And when I spoke of love and joy, not a word was
    understood.
"And yet in church they sing their hymns and whisper
    up their prayers.

"Then they all go out and fight again. They literally split
hairs!"

"Yet there are a few in that dark place who really love
our Lord.
"They walk close to His side with their lives based on
His Word.
"They daily strive for Christian love, and I thrilled to
hear them sing
"About His birth in Bethlehem, giving honor to our
King.

"But they're a minority in that place; real Christians
there are rare.
"I tell you, they're killing each other off in that crazy
world down there!
"Something must be done there very soon! That world's
about to blow!
"Maybe next year at Christmastime, our Lord Himself
should go!"

EMMANUEL

Tiny Baby, fair of face;
Fulfillment of God's promised grace.
Majestic Homeland left behind;
The Messiah is clothed as humankind.

Hear the mother softly sing
A lullaby to Heaven's King.
On the straw, 'midst ox and sheep,
The Prince of Peace lies fast asleep.

An angel choir; a glorious Star,
Eastern kings who journeyed far;
With joy, the shepherds, their story tell:
"He has come; Emmanuel!"

God with us; oh, wondrous thought!
To earth, salvation has been brought!
Hear, all ye people; the anthem swell!
God's with us! Emmanuel!

Behold, a virgin shall be with child, and shall bring forth a
son, and they shall call his name Emmanuel, which being in-
terpreted is, God with us.

—Matthew 1:23

BROWNIE GOES TO BETHLEHEM

"Mama, aren't we almost there?" the little donkey
    sighed.
"For we have come a long, long way, and my feet are
    very tired."

"Hush, now, child," his mama said. "It's not much far-
    ther now.
"My lady needs a place to sleep and rest her weary brow.
"I've carried her from Nazareth, for she is great with
    child.
"So we must get to Bethlehem; then we can rest awhile."

So, little Brownie trotted on, close to big Gray's side,
Watching as the sky grew dim and day neared eventide.
It had not been a joyous trip—too many angry men,
Who'd shake their fists in Caesar's face for what he'd
    done to them!
And soon a call from up ahead: "Bethlehem's o'er the
    hill!"
Within the city's gates, at last, the caravan stood still.

There were angry people everywhere, with not a vacant
    bed!

Poor tired lady and weary man, no place to lay their
heads.

"Mama, whatever shall we do? The lady's very white.

"I fear she'll fall from off your back! Will no one help
tonight?"

"I don't know, child," the mama said. "There are many
people here."

But then an innkeeper shouted out, "My stable's in the
rear!"

Big Gray and Brownie stood, at last, within the stable's
walls,

And just in time, for birth's travail, the lady, did befall.

The Child was wrapped so lovingly and placed upon the
hay.

"Mama, just look how small He is! I could carry Him all
day!"

"Yes, child, He is a little One—" Just then the door
swung wide

And shepherds crying, "Praise to God," rushed to the
Baby's side!

They knelt in humble reverence and told the strangest
tale.

That angels had sung of God's own Son being born in
Bethlehem's vale.

"Mama, whatever do they mean? Is He the promised
  One?

"Mama, I must get close to see our dear Creator's Son!"

So, little Brownie crept up to the lowly manger bed.

The lady reached out her loving hand to pat him on the
  head.

He looked the Baby up and down and felt his heart
  o'erflow.

The Majesty, from Heaven's realm, had come to earth
  below.

"Mama! Mama! This is Him! Oh, Mama, come and see!

"They have called Him, 'Jesus,' Mama! Come, see Him
  look at me!"

Big Gray stood close to Brownie's side, in awe, with
  heads bowed low.

To think that they had been a part of prophecy foretold!

That He would come, and here He was! The earth His
  feet would trod!

This tiny Babe, so pure and sweet, was Heaven's incar-
  nate God!

WHAT CHRISTMAS MEANS TO ME

A brilliant star, an angel choir,
Shepherds tending sheep.
A sheltering shed, a manger bed,
Bethlehem, asleep.

A Baby's cry, soft lullaby,
A mother's gentle voice.
Eastern kings, their presents bring;
Heaven and Earth, rejoice.

From Heaven's home, our Lord has come;
With men, He now will dwell.
The Infant King, salvation brings;
He is here! Emmanuel!

EASTER

How sad it was on that fateful day;
Jesus, in a tomb, did lay.
The Sun hid her eyes in a cloud so dark;
No sound could be heard from the little Lark.

The Earth groaned and trembled. "Oh, what has Man
      done
To our Creator's only Son?"
The Wind came and whistled in a note so shrill,
"What's going on, on Calvary's hill?"

The Lily replied, as she drew in her head,
"The only Begotten of the Father is dead."
And as, in Joseph's tomb, He lay,
The World shed tears of grief that day.

For three days and nights the old World cried.
Jesus, the King, for man, had died.
The World withdrew; its beauty was gone;
For how could it sing when its heart was torn?

That morning the Sun came out to see.
For how could such a strange thing be?
The Wind had reported an angel, bright,

Had descended to Earth, in raiment white.

The stone from the tomb, he rolled away,
And up rose Jesus, from whence He lay!
Alive! A Victor o'er the grave!
Alive! Man's sinful soul to save!

The Lily raised her weeping head
To welcome Jesus from the dead.
The gentle Breeze caressed His face;
The Lark sang sweetly of His grace.

The Earth brought out her song once more.
The victory's won; the battle's o'er.
The babbling Water sweetly sings,
"He lives! He lives! Our priestly King!"

THE WARRIOR

He came by humble stable; indeed, it wasn't grand.
People could not see Him as the Savior of their land.
His clothes were not of royal hue; He bore no warrior's
shield.
How He could ever help them was more than they could
feel.

"Why He's teaching brotherhood and love for every
man?
"What we need is a fighter, who'll come and free our
land."
"We want a mighty warrior," the people loudly cried.
And He, their great Redeemer, they took and crucified.

They're still looking for their warrior; their Messiah,
long foretold.
How sad they did not know Him, when He came so long
ago.
He's coming back some happy day to conquer all the
world.
He'll return this time to reign, with banners all unfurled.

This time, He'll be a warrior; victory shouts will ring.
He'll be our great Deliverer, our Conqueror and King!

ALONE FOR ME

I saw Him at Praetorian's Hall; His friends did from
    Him flee.
The howling mob cried for His blood, and alone, He
    stood for me.
At a distance, from where I stood, His face, I could not
    see.
Tired, He seemed, but not afraid, and, oh, so alone was
    He.

On top of Calvary's rugged hill, they nailed Him to a
    tree.
And as precious drops of blood rolled down, alone He
    died for me.
Alone when condemned; alone in death; yet He tri-
    umphed o'er the foe.
He arose a victor o'er the grave to save man's dying soul.

Because He lives, I shall live, too. 'Tis the sweetest
    thought to me.
When through death's shadowed vale I trod, this Friend
    will walk with me.
He said He would never leave my side; never alone I'd
    be.

But a picture I see of Praetorian's Hall and how, all
    alone, was He.

Oh, may I never Thee deny; may I Thy witness be.
May I hold Thy bloodstained banner high and say, "It
    was for me"!

MIDNIGHT AND DAWN

On Calvary's hill many years ago, one bleak and lonely
day,
Some people watched as all hope died and in Joseph's
tomb was laid.
Shaken spirits and sorrowing hearts; tears filled every
eye;
The same sad question rose in every mind: "Why did
Jesus have to die?"

He who had been so loving and kind to all He chanced
to meet.
And now, here He lay, in death's deep rest, with scars
on His hands and feet.
Why did He die? Why did He die? He, who was their
King!
They left the garden feeling quite alone, and nobody
thought to sing.

Their midnight had come, and all was dark. Who could
think of the dawn?
But, as surely as night does roll around, even surely,
comes the morn.
To the tomb quite early, after a day of rest. 'Twas the
last thing they could do.

They would embalm His body with spices sweet and bid
   Him "Farewell" anew.

The stone at the tomb presented a task for the women
   all alone.
But to their surprise, as they drew near, they saw that
   it was gone.
Wonder and amazement their beings filled, as a Man in
   white did say,
"Why seek ye the living among the dead? Behold, He
   lives today!"

The empty tomb bespoke the truth of the words the angel said.
Their hearts did thrill at the words divine: "He is risen
   from the dead!"
With wings on their feet, they ran to tell the story that
   has never grown old.
"He has risen as He said He would!" Sweetest story ever
   told!

IT HAD TO BE

The angel band stood close at hand by God the Father's
throne.
Not one stirred; none spoke a word. In Heaven, grief
was known.
Their eyes transfixed into Earth's midst, where stood a
lonely Man.
He stood alone, with friends all gone; none offered Him
their hand.

Condemned to die for you and I, and nailed upon a tree.
As they boasted proud, He cried aloud, "Why hast Thou
forsaken Me?"
An angel spoke low, "Master, shall we go, and take Him
from the cross?
"We'll stop their mirth, destroy the Earth, and leave
them in darkness gross."

God answered, "No, you must not go. He knows what
must be done.
"I'll turn my eye that He may die. The victory must be
won."
God looked away that awful day and allowed His Son
to die.

For a sinning race that sought not His face, nor upon
>   His name did cry.

Then shall He not count every drop of blood falling
>   from the tree?
A redemption plan for fallen man—He knew it had to
>   be.

TELL ME AGAIN OF CALVARY

Tell me again of Calvary. Are you sure it was for me?
You say it was a King that died and bore such agony?
You say there are nail prints in His hands and a spear-
    wound in His side?
Angry stripes upon His back and on Calvary, crucified?

That for the sins of a wicked world, His blood flowed
    down that tree?
Redemption for the captive souls? But was there enough
    for me?
For I am black with the stains of sins, no righteous per-
    son here.
Yet I am weary with sin's dark night. I need a friend to
    care.

You say His name is Jesus? God's Son from Heaven
    above,
And was in my place, sacrificed? I've never known such
    love!
Please tell me again of Calvary, of how I can be free
From all my sin and guilt and fear. Please tell it again
    to me!

THE FOUNTAIN

A Fountain was opened some years ago outside a city,
    fair.
Out on a hillside, bleak and gray, instead of the city's
    square.
They used no polished marble stone, but fashioned it
    from wood.
And, as on any opening day, people came to where it
    stood.

There to behold, 'midst all the noise, not the usual
    figurines,
But the figure of a lonely Man in a somber, deathlike
    scene.
No fresh, clear, sparkling waters were splashing all
    around.
But t'was a deep red, crimson stream that stained the
    wood and ground.

When it was done, it was back to town except for just
    a few,
Who stayed to cry, who understood the significance of
    the view.
For many years the fount has stood neglected, criticized.

For it's kind of off the beaten path; the crowds just pass
      it by.

But those who turn aside to wash in its redeeming flow
Have found it cleansed the deepest stains from their
      immortal soul.
They've gone to tell of its saving power to whosoever
      will.
Let all men come and enter in; the stream is flowing
      still.

The Word has gone around the world, from mountain-
      top declared.
There's a fountain opened to the House of David out-
      side a city, fair.

*In that day there shall be a fountain opened to the house of
David and to the inhabitants of Jerusalem for sin and for
uncleanness.*

                         —Zechariah 13:1

THE VEIL

I heard their joyous worship, their singing and their
      praise,
The blowing of the shofar on their high holy days.
I longed to know about their God and tried to look
      within,
But He had placed a veil between and I could not enter
      in.

The veil was thick and ominous; it shrouded every view.
And though I tried, there was no door to let me pass on
      through.
Outside their camp, a Voice rang out. "It is finished!"
      was His cry,
And the shadow of a cross appeared between the veil
      and I.

I looked away to Calvary's hill and saw the ground
      stained red.
The sky above turned black as night; the ground be-
      neath me fled.
I heard a thunderous, rending sound and looked above
      to see
The veil was torn from sky to ground by the Man of
      Calvary.

A trail of blood from Calvary's cross led through the veil
within.
And I heard the Voice of their Mighty God saying, "All
may enter in."
I arose, and through His blood I stepped inside the veil.
I joined with them in praise to God for the Lamb that
did prevail.

And now I stand as one of them, redeemed from every
sin.
The Veil is gone through Christ my Lord. With joy, I've
entered in.

ANNIVERSARY

Dearest Bob,

If I should have ten thousand pens
And know the language of all men;
Keys to open every door;
And a mind that all things could explore.

Yet I could never find a way
To tell you all my love today.
A love that grows and grows and grows
And blossoms sweeter than the rose.

And tho each door I'd look behind
I don't believe I'd ever find
Words that would begin to tell
The story my heart knows so well.

So, you must only try to guess
The words my tongue just can't express.
And know how boundless, free, and true
Are simple words, like "I love you"!

Linda

TO MY LOVE

If I shouldst tell thee how I love thee
Thou wouldst ne'er believe the words!
Upon thine ears t'would be melody sweeter
Than the singing of the birds.

My lips would drop with golden nectar;
Mine eyes would dance with fire;
If I could tell thee how thou art
All things my heart desires.

Two flirting eyes, so deep and brown;
A crooked smile and grin;
Muscles to rival those of a god;
Combine my heart to win.

Higher than heights; deeper than depths;
So great my love for thee.
To be in thine arms; to hear of thy love;
'Tis where I long to be.

So, on and on, till length of days
Only thine, my love shall be.
Till in death's peace, mine eyes do close
My heart shall beat for thee.

TO FALL IN LOVE

Moonbeams drifting through the treetops
Resting on your raven hair;
Love and beauty; witchery and madness
Met my gaze and held me there.

Last night I walked as one who dreams,
Who is led away to rapturous shores
And there tastes of forbidden glory;
A transient glimpse through other doors.

The night-winds played their bewitching song;
The moon cast a magic spell
And made the earth an enchanted garden,
A beauteous spot where lovers dwell.

With your gentle caress and tender lips
You led my heart away
To a realm that mortals only know
When joyous love has come to stay.

THE VOYAGE

My starship broke all earthly ties
And sailed through dark, majestic skies.
Through Milky Way; past golden stars;
My fiery ship could know no bars.

Winging free 'neath Heaven's dome;
Each tiny port was now my home.
Spirit unfurled, with naught in mind;
Except to roam in scenes sublime.

What was the reason for my trip?
Why did I choose from Earth to slip?
To visit Mercury; Venus; Mars:
To freely walk among the stars?

Your lips on mine, so full of love
Had sent my heart to heights above;
To stroll through space with no alarms
As I lay nestled in your arms.

GOD SAW US THROUGH

When we were married, Dad and me,
We were as poor as church mice be.
But we had love, the kind that's true
And our God always saw us through.

A little cottage on a hill;
A little patch of ground to till;
To us it seemed that Heaven had loaned
A spot that mortals could call their own.

We raised our brood with sweat and tears.
Our prayers have followed them through the years.
The nights we slept sometimes were few.
But God has always brought us through.

There were feverish hours when death seemed nigh.
The doctor would shake his head and sigh,
And say, "There's naught that I can do."
But God was there to see us through.

Some years no fruit came from the ground;
The food didn't want to stretch around
But we thanked God for what we had.
We've weathered both good times and bad.

Dad's coal-black hair is mixed with gray;
He looks quite dignified that way.
After years together, he's destined, it seems,
To always be the man of my dreams.

There were hills we climbed the hard way.
We quarreled, when we knew to pray.
But our love is deep and strong and true;
And our God has always seen us through.

MY SAPPHIRE BABY

Born in September, the month of blue;
He's my Sapphire Baby, through and through.

A true-blue gent, this man of mine;
But he can feed you quite a line.

He's very good-looking, hardheaded, and sweet;
And his kiss can sweep me off my feet!

 I love his eyes; his crooked grin;
The shape of his head; and his bearded chin.

I love him dearly, but then, just maybe
It's simply because he's my Sapphire Baby!

THE OLD PREACHER

The old gray-headed preacher arose from off the seat;
He started toward the sacred desk, unsteady on his feet.
He used a cane and held on tight; his hands with palsy
shook;
His eyes were dim; he couldn't read the scriptures from
the Book.
His speech was halted; yet he knew the truths that lay
within
The covers of that precious book could cleanse the
deepest sin!

His heart had once been black as night; he had known
the depths of shame.
But through the cross, he'd been redeemed, and his
soul was set aflame!
The chains that held him fast were gone; Christ Jesus
set him free!
His name was in the Book of Life for all eternity!
The Lord would soon return for us; it could be any day;
The time grew short; soon He'd appear to catch His
Bride away.

A few more words, and he returned to sit down once
again.

And you knew by the way he spoke that Jesus was his
    Friend.
Each day he walked and talked with Him, though pain-
    ful was the way.
Soon he and Jesus would talk it over in Heaven's eternal
    day.
No need of cane; no tremors there; clearness of eyes
    and voice.
He'll join the choir in redemption's song, forever to
    rejoice.

MY HUSBAND—A GIFT FROM GOD

My husband if a gift from God, direct from Him to me.
I couldn't have picked a better one; he suits me perfectly!
He's a little rough around the edges; sometimes his
    temper flares.
But he says he has a reason; I gave him those gray hairs!

We don't always see eye to eye. Sometimes we disagree.
And we have those loud "discussions" when he refuses
    my point to see!
But we have weathered all the storms; we've seen good
    times and bad.
There have been times we really felt that "we" were all
    we had!

He'd hold my hand or hold me close and say, "It will be
    okay."
I've leaned on that shoulder many times and knew there
    would be a way.
I can't say I've always been the best of wives, you know.
But what would I do without him? Forget it! I don't
    want to know!

His faith in God and his trust in me have helped me on
    my way.

He truly is my gift from God. And I wish him a "happy birthday"!

THE JOURNEY

You left me standing there, quite forlorn, in front of a
    country store;
The sky was black with approaching storm and evening
    closed her door.
"You cannot come," you said to me. "I must go on alone.
"Meet me over on the other side." And with that, you
    were gone.
The mountain road was narrow and steep, very dark
    and overgrown.
Treacherous curves and deep ravines—all threatened
    your journey home.

I watched you struggle to make your way, ofttimes with
    little light.
I cried when evening's soft, gray mist turned into dark-
    est night.
It was hard to relinquish the driver's seat; but at last it
    had to be.
An unseen Hand took hold of the wheel, to bring you
    home to me.
And though I waited so many days, you did not return
    to me.
God knew that you were growing tired, and He whis-
    pered, "Come with Me."

I thought I could not bear the pain when in death you
closed your eyes.
But in my heart, I heard you say, "Meet me over on the
other side."
And so, in spite of many long, long hours, the tears have
dropped like rain,
I am prepared and awaiting the day when I'll see you
again.
So, don't go too fast now; wait for me! With you, I want
to abide,
Through eternity's day, with Jesus our Lord, over on the
other side.

TWO FEET

Two feet:
Small and wrapped in booties, blue;
They kick with joy at Mother's coo;
They learn to walk in brand-new shoes.

Two feet:
Barefoot or shod, they run around;
Up in tall trees they can be found;
Or sliding on winter's frozen ground.

Two feet:
Off to school or hard at play;
Growing larger every day;
Choosing paths along the way.

Two feet:
Combat boots they may acquire;
Or steel-toed shoes for mud and mire;
Or plushy-softs when hot and tired.

Two feet:
Walk down the aisle on a wedding day;
Kneel with little ones to pray;
Walking in the paths of God always.

Two feet:
Once so strong, now halt in stride;
May stumble and fall without a guide;
Now shuffle slowly to the other side.

Two feet:
Pass on through death's darkened door;
And enter Heaven's golden shore;
To walk up there forevermore.

Two feet:
They walk with Jesus' pierced feet;
With angels down the golden street;
And live in peace, sublime and sweet.

IN HIS PRESENCE

I laid my head in Jesus' lap; He gently stroked my hair.
It was so good to be near Him and know He truly cared.
He wiped away the stinging tears that fell like drench-
    ing rain.
His comforting presence cheered my soul and helped to
    ease my pain.

He let me stay there till the sobs that wracked my soul
    had passed.
I heard Him say with gentle voice, "Dear one, this storm
    won't last.
"It will soon be only a memory in a heart that's growing
    strong.
"The clouds and rain will soon give way to glorious
    praise and song."

The storm still raged, but peace had come; His love
    would be my stay.
I stood to my feet, clothed with His strength, and knew
    I could face the day.
Many storms of life have come and gone, and each time
    my battered soul
Takes refuge kneeling at His feet; His love does make
    me whole.

PREACHER'S DAUGHTER

"My mother is a preacher." That phrase brought gales
    of laughter
From kids who didn't understand how serious was the
    matter.
"You can't do this!" "You can't do that!" "You can't go
    here nor there!"
"What kind of life are you living? How dull! How bor-
    ing! How drear!"

Dull? Boring? Drear? Well, maybe yes—but maybe not!
Maybe God has blessed me with something they've not
    got.
Ere I had learned to toddle, I knew there was a God.
And each night she sang a hymn as my head began to
    nod.

She taught me early how to pray and to read God's Holy
    Word.
She showed me by example that faith will turn the
    sword.
Twice as death overtook me, her prayers held me to this
    side.
She put her trust in God above and stemmed the raging
    tide.

Her prayers and trust surround us as we walk life's vale
of tears.
I'm the luckiest person in the world! My mother really
cares!
Yes, Mother is a preacher! The road's been hard to trod.
But unfailing faith and courage brave have kept her
true to God.

I'm glad she chose to obey God and not pay heed to man.
What would I do had she not taught me how to hold
God's hand?

MY DAD

A dad I have as most folks do, but none other's quite
    like mine!
For the mold was broken after him and cancelled out
    that line.
He's a little short, with not much hair; his eyes an azure
    blue.
Sometimes they laugh; sometimes they don't; depend-
    ing on what I do.

He's always gone by "Duffy," although that's not his
    name.
But it's as Irish as his Irish temper, which no one's ever
    tamed.
His tongue can turn the air quite blue and leaves most
    folks aghast.
When he's around, you're never sure what next from
    his lips will pass.

"The Wit and Wisdom of Duffy" would be banned, if up
    for sale.
But, oh, there's times it hits the head of that proverbial
    nail!
What do you do with a dad like mine? You take him as
    he is!

For underneath all that bluff and bluster, I know he's
glad I'm his.

He might never say he was proud of me, but I know it
anyway.
He seems to find that mushy stuff is kind of hard to say.
But when I needed him, he was there. He'd take good
care of me.
For he's my dad and I'm his daughter; and we love us,
don't you see.

THE HOMEWARD JOURNEY

"Honey, let's go to Indiana." That's music to my ears!
We've been away from home and friends for many a
passing year.
Oh, the excitement that's in the air as we pack and plan
away!
Forty dozen things that must be done getting ready for
the day.

Minor details, small frustrations, never dim the joy
within.
I know in just a few more days I'll see the kith and kin.
Finally, we pile into the car, and down the road we start.
I ride the many weary miles with wings upon my heart.

With my mind's eye I look ahead and see them as before:
Daddy looking through the window, Mama waiting by
the door.
And as I wend my homeward way, a parallel I see,
Between this journey and another to my home in
eternity.

For that one, too, I'm making plans, getting ready now
to go.

I've got the ticket bought for me by the Lamb's redeeming flow.
And though sometimes the getting ready is fraught
with stinging tears,
I still feel excitement in the air as I know the day draws
near.

Soon the redeemed of all the ages will hear that silvery
sound.
We'll pile on board that Gospel Train; at last, we're
Homeward bound!
And as, by faith, I look ahead, I see them waiting there;
Beside the gates they watch for me to enter Heaven fair.
And so I wend my homeward way with joy deep in my
heart.
Soon I'll be with the kith and kin for eternity, ne'er to
part.

THE SOUNDING OF THE BELL

It's Sunday morning, and I hear a distant church bell
    ring.
It sounds so clear, and to my heart sweet memories it
    brings.
I journey back in reverie to far-off yesterdays,
To other Sunday mornings in a place so far away.

I see a dark-haired little girl with laughing blue-gray
    eyes,
Walking down a country road beneath an azure sky.
On her way to a little church on a hill above the dell.
Out through the fresh, clear morning resounds its ring-
    ing bell.

I watch the people enter in and fill each empty pew.
Sweet faces from the distant past go passing in review.
There's Mother dear, who now has gone to that Celes-
    tial Land.
How many times I climbed that hill while holding to her
    hand.

There's Grandma Hardwick; Riggle-Mom; there's Jim
    and Minnie, too.

Dear Aunt Eunice; Sister Moore; Lois; Matt; and Grandma Hughes.

Their voices raise in melodious song to their eternal
King.

It seems that Heaven answers back, and I hear the angels sing.

Through open doors and windows, the soft, cool breez-
es blow

And waft the sounds of joyous praise through all the
vale below.

Breaking through my reverie are tears upon my face.

I yearn to stay a longer while in this remembered place.

But there will come another time when those from
yesteryear

Will sing their song through Heaven's day, their voices
strong and clear.

And I will greet them on that shore where the blessed
will ever dwell,

When all the saints are gathered in at the sounding of
the bell.

KAREN MARRIES SAM

She came down the aisle, all dressed up in white,
A vision of beauty and charm.
Shaky, weak knees and butterfly stomach,
Supported by Daddy's strong arm.

With bright shining eyes and face all aglow,
She weds this young man in blue.
In the joy of the hour, she clearly forgets
The tissues stuffed in each shoe.

The ceremony is sweet, with friends all around.
 "See, everything turned out just right!"
Though preparations went wild and her wedding cake
        leans,
She still is the star of the night!

Another daughter I have, who someday will wed
A shining knight of her dreams, I hope.
But I think I may say, "Here's the keys to the car.
"There's a full tank of gas—elope!"

BABY'S SLEEPY LAND

Mr. Sandman came with his magic sand to make his
    nightly round.
He sprinkled some in your sweet, bright eyes, and their
    covers fluttered down.
When they lay fast on rosy cheeks, he took you by the
    hand
And whisked you away to the dreamy world of a baby's
    Sleepy Land.

Dimpled smile and puckered lips play hopscotch on
    your face
As you watch the tiny folk at play in this enchanted
    place.
Blue-gowned fairies with gossamer wings catch moon-
    beams in their hand,
And dance on the rims of buttercups to music from an
    elfin band.

A bunch of gremlins join the dance and scare them all
    away.
But soon they leave and once again the wee folk come
    to play.
Soon playtime ends in this magic place where fairies
    dance, and then,

The covers lift from rosy cheeks, and you are home
again.

MY GRANDSON, ROBERT

"I'm hungry," says this plaintive voice that bounces
 through my door,
Dribbling basketball and tennies beating tattoos on my
 floor.
The ever-present baseball cap covers sun-kissed hair,
Knee-knocker shorts and big T-shirt—a vision of
 savior-faire!

"Whatcha got that's good to eat?" is the question of the
 day.
With eyes lit up by heaven's blue, my fridge gets a quick
 foray.
He has breakfast, lunch, and dinner, and ten snacks in
 between.
But the hollow leg is still not filled on this fine-tuned
 eating machine.

Chips and sodas or roasted pigs; baloney or apple pie!
As long as it doesn't eat him first, he'll give it all a try!
So, don't be long with all that food! Don't wait that meat
 to carve!
Just bring it on and fill him up! This kid's about to
 starve!

BABY KISSES

He gives out a long, low whistle;
She knows that little tweet!
She lifts her chubby, little arms;
He sweeps her off her feet.

Her cherub face lights up with smiles;
Both hands go for his beard.
She giggles and gurgles and babbles away.
To her grandpa, the words are clear.

With her flashing eyes and drippy chin
And a mouth that never misses,
She wets his face with sugary drool
And gives her grandpa dirty kisses.

He wipes off the drool and makes a face,
But it really makes his day,
When Baby wets his whiskers down
In her own sweet, drippy way.

MY GRANDDAUGHTER, ASHLEY

What's that music that I hear
Falling softly on my ear?
Silvery sounds that fall, and seem
As a rushing, flowing stream.

Like a melody from the hills
Tripping over rocks and rills,
Lifting now above the trees,
Falling softly on the leas.

Wafting through the forest glen,
Hushed, and then resounds again,
The source of music on the wing?
It's the sound of Ashley laughing!

A RIDE WITH KAREN

Are there demons chasing us?
Dark spirits I don't see?
Or maybe someone has a gun,
And for our lives we flee!

Could it be an alarm was raised?
Are they coming by land or sea?
Are they pursuing us just now?
But what else can it be?

But, no; I settle back into the seat
And just enjoy the ride.
As people, houses, other cars,
And trees go flying by.

Zipping past them all, are we!
See, I am brave and daring!
I never went so far, so fast,
As the day I rode with Karen!

BOBBI

My dearest Bobbi,

I said a prayer for you today,
That God would brighten all your way.
I knew your heart was bowed with care
And so I went to God in prayer.
I saw you struggle with your load
And walk along a lonely road.

I prayed He would your strength renew
And make your smile to shine anew.
I saw that rain dwelled in your eyes
And prayed for golden, sunny skies.
When fall the stinging tears of grief,
I prayed that He would send relief.

When doubts and fears cause you alarm,
May He enfold you in His arms.
'Midst all the trials that you face,
May you feel His love and grace.

When dawns are gray and hope seems gone,
May you know you are His own;
Secured in love that's ever true.

Beloved child, I prayed for you.

Love, Mom

SUMMER'S WEDDING

The date was July the twenty-fifth;
The year was two thousand and four.
And on this day, sweet Summer's Bride
Was standing at the door.

She was gowned in white from head to toe;
She carried a rose bouquet.
From the aura of radiance that covered her,
Your breath was caught away.

She'd waited so long for this day to arrive,
And now its fulfillment was here.
For standing inside by the altar of God
Was the man who loved her so dear.

She entered the door; the music began,
Escorted to stand by his side.
There were songs and rings and promises made,
In eternal love to abide.

Dark days are forgotten; tomorrow is bright;
All tears of loneliness past.
The whispered "I do" begins a new day
For John Joe and Bobbi at last.

JOHN

He carefully hung his cowboy hat on the back of a
    wooden chair
He was tall and dark and very lean with salt-and-pepper
    hair.
His body had been wracked with sickness; he had tast-
    ed the depths of sin.
For years he ran from the voice of God, till Jesus brought
    him in.

The call of God is now on his life; the mantle he had long
    denied,
As an invisible cloak surrounds him now and is worn
    with godly pride.
He, whom Satan had meant to destroy, nearly taking
    his life away,
Has been ordained for a time such as this and is speak-
    ing here today.

No eloquent speech; just gospel truth; in the language
    of the street.
Jesus is all he'd ever needed; He has made his life
    complete.
Through sorrow and pain, trials and tears, he's found
    the Homeward track;

The road ahead leads only to God; there now is no looking back.

A deep, abiding faith in God's power, a belief for impossible things,
Will keep him true to the call of God and lead him to where angels sing.

BOB AND JOSHUA

Now, tell me quickly, baby dear, while your thoughts of
    Heaven are clear,
Before you left its streets so fair, did you see Great-
    Grandpa there?
He just had gone before you came, but I am sure he
    knew your name!
Did he hold you in a fond embrace and kiss your tiny
    baby face?

And did he smile that crooked grin when you touched
    his bearded chin?
Did he lift you high up in the air or dance with you on
    golden stairs?
I know that he was well and strong as he lovingly car-
    ried you along;
And said, "It's time for you to go your way; you must
    help brighten all their day.

"Please give each one of them my love and say I'm
    watching from above.
"It won't be long till you'll all be home, and we'll laugh
    and sing around the throne."
I know he kissed you one more time as you left Heav-
    en's sunny clime.

So, before you forget, while thoughts are clear, please
tell me quickly, baby dear!

THE LITTLE WARRIOR

The forest halls are silent; the dragons come no more.
The whip-poor-wills now sing their song as evening
shuts her door.
The ghosts and goblins hide away; the bears run to their
dens.
They hurry away from the mighty arrows that the little
warrior sends.

From early morn till set of sun, he battled among them
all.
Routing all that came to his door down through the forest hall.
His bow was sure; his arrows true; and Mama now is
safe.
For all who would come and harm them, he securely put
away.

And now the sun is setting; dusk, now, o'er all does
creep.
He rests his tiny head on Mama; little Joshua is asleep.

MICHELLE

Is that Michelle? IT IS MICHELLE!
I thought some fairy princess
    With golden hair and blue, blue eyes
    Had dropped from Heaven's sunny skies,
To teach me again what love is!

I love that sweet, mischievous grin,
The smiles that light your face.
    They come like sunshine after rain;
    They cause my heart to sing again
And brighten all my cloudy days.

A bundle of energy, on the go!
Do your feet ever touch the ground?
    You flit like a butterfly on the wing,
    Eagerly searching into everything!
Grand, new treasures to be found.

Little Michelle; my sweet Michelle!
Even though you're not quite three,
    Always remember wherever you go,
    That Gigi Linda loves you so!
You mean the world to me!

SOPHIA

Sophia! Sophia! Child of grace!
You've made my world a sunny place!
Bursting in upon our lives
With giggly grins and laughing eyes.

You stole my love with the first embrace,
As I kissed your tiny cherub face.
Then as you toddled with a baby's art,
You left your footprints on my heart.

God has blessed me once again
With the greatest joy of tongue or pen.
Sophia! Sophia! Child of grace!
You've made my world a sunny place!

ANGEL TEARS

Another loved one laid to rest;
Again, the sorrow's deep.
Haunting memories flood our souls
And bitter tears we weep.

Raindrops from the heavens
Mingle with our tears.
They fall as softly on the ground
As ours do on the bier.

I've heard it said the angels
Who watch us here below
Are deeply troubled by our grief
And their eyes with tears o'er-flow.

Raindrops are naught but crystal tears
From Heaven's portals shed,
For our God, He knows each heartache
As we walk behind the dead.

So, when we see the rain fall
We know our God will keep.
And as we cry, remember,
The angels also weep.

IN MEMORY OF MOM

I sure would like to hug your neck
And say, "I love you, Mom."
And wish you bright and sunny days
For many years to come.

But you're away on that bright shore
Where days are always fair.
I know that God will give to you
A "Happy Birthday" over there.

IN MEMORIAM

Sleeping in God! A wondrous thought!
But sorrow to our hearts it brought.
One long and lonely year today,
Angel wings bore you away.
With broken hearts and tear-filled eyes,
We vowed we'd meet you in the skies.
How sad 'twould be, if we'd not meet
Upon some lovely golden street.
May Jesus help us to prepare,
For by His grace, we'll meet you there.

IN MEMORY

The vacant chair; the silent voice;
The face we see no more;
To us are loving memories
Of one gone on before.

In peaceful sleep he now doth rest;
For him, life's story's told.
He's gone to sing redemption's song,
In a land where he'll never grow old.

A MEMORY

The wind blows softly o'er the sod.
But you're not there; you're at home with God.
Sleeping sweetly on His breast;
'Tis a comfort to know you are at rest.

A GOOD NIGHT PRAYER

Jesus, I've come to say "Good night."
Thank You for the day so bright.
Bless those I love
From Heaven above,
And keep us through the night.
Amen.

CHILDHOOD

Running barefoot through the grass;
Wading water, clear as glass;
Wiling away sweet summer's hours
In a garden filled with flowers.

Catching June bugs on the wing;
Taking a nap on the old porch swing;
Running with dogs; playing with cats;
Trying on Mother's shoes and hats.

Picking apples from a gnarled old tree;
Hiding from wasps and bumblebees;
Watching the little chickens hatch;
Taking a bucket to the berry patch.

Playing Hide-and-Seek at night;
Watching the firefly's backup light;
And when autumn's song is sung,
Catching snowflakes on my tongue.

Hearing the call of the whip-poor-will;
Or sledding down a snowy hill;
In frosty winters or summers mild,
Oh, what fun to be a child!

IT'S FALL

Mother Nature's dressed again
In lovely, rustling gowns.
Splotches here and there of golds,
And reds, and greens, and browns.
  It's fall.

Harvest moon and fodder shock;
Ripe pumpkin on the vine;
For pies and Jack-o'-lanterns, too
On Halloween to shine.
  It's fall.

Bulging barns and cellar shelves;
All winter stores piled high.
Old Tom Turkey, unaware,
Thanksgiving Day is nigh.
  It's fall.

Sweaters, caps, and frosty breaths;
Mornings, crisp and clear.
Beautiful days of Indian summer,
And wintertime is near.
  It's fall.

SNOW IN BROWNSVILLE, TEXAS

"Elfin, where'd we put the snow?" Old Man Winter
   cried.
"I had boxed up some for all points south and put it to
   the side.
"I've found the boxes for the north and east; and the
   west is set to go.
"But what in the world did we do with that box of southern snow?
"I think that Brownsville, Texas, might really like some
   snow.
"After that blistering summer heat; a treat for them,
   you know.

"But all I've found for them so far is wind and drizzly
   rain.
"And that just lasts a day or two, then the heat's turned
   on again.
"It doesn't seem like wintertime without some snow
   around.
"But if I don't find that southern box, there'll be none
   on their ground.
"Well, it seems I have no choice; it's half past fall, you
   know.

"I can't put winter off much longer. But I'd sure like to
find that snow!"

Elfin gleefully danced around the box because he knew
full well,
That never was there a snowflake made that could stand
the heat of Hell!
But Old Man Winter saw him there; he grabbed the box
and ran.
Through the window, he threw the box toward the
south's warm land.
Flakes of snow began to fall, and by Christmas Day's
first light,
All the streets of Brownsville, Texas, were clothed in
winter's white.

Every person, young and old, with awed delights looked
on
As an inch and a half of fresh snow fell and glistened in
the dawn.
Snowmen popped up everywhere—even on trunks of
cars!
Snowball fights, snow angels, too; this Christmas was
the best, by far!
Old Man Winter watched and laughed. "Who said it
couldn't be?

"Maybe in another hundred years, it'll happen again!
We'll see!"

Note: On December 24, 2004, at 10:00 p.m., it started snowing in Brownsville, Texas, for the first time in 109 years! By Christmas morning, there was an inch and a half of snow on the ground that stayed for two days.

RAINBOWS IN MY SINK

Colorful rainbows in my sink!
Every sunny morn I see
These rainbows in my kitchen sink;
They're smiling up at me.

And when I see their vivid hues,
I remember the vow of God.
No more would He destroy the Earth
With waters from a flood.

Four thousand years have come and gone,
And yet His promise stands.
Then can I doubt that I'll receive
My promises at His hands?

So, come on, Rainbows; shine for me!
I know God's Word is true!
These rainbows in my kitchen sink
Say my God will come through!

THE SUNBEAM

Hello, Sunbeam! I see you there,
Clinging playfully to my wall!
You sneaked in through my windowpane
And came to pay a call.

To dance around on golden feet
And toss your streaming hair
Against the wall; behind the door;
I see you hiding there!

I bid you welcome, Golden Spot,
Tiny offspring of the Sun.
So, come on in and stay awhile;
The morning's just begun!

Highlight with lovely, lacy gold
The décor of this room.
Let your dazzling, shimmering brilliance
Chase away the gloom.

Now, why are you dimming, Little Spot?
It's time to leave, you say?
Well, remember where my window is
And call another day.

VANS

Vans to the left of me! Vans to the right of me!
What's a little Grand Am to do?
I've flicked my lights and honked my horn
And still I can't get through!

These monoliths prowl every road
At speeds that cramp my style!
I've been behind these big taillights
For mile after weary mile!

I watch for even the slightest hole
That might let me get through.
But I'm boxed in, with no way out;
So, what am I going to do?

If I see even the tiniest chance
For passing in my view;
My tires will scream, "Now, look out, Van!
"This Pontiac is coming through!"

CENTRAL SUPPLY

Bedpans, urinals, and paper caps;
Specimen cups and masks.
Need a catheter? Any size!
Just call C.S. and ask!

Brushes and bottles of this and that;
Syringes and needles galore!
IV pumps; suction machines;
We're like a general store!

Water and tapes and clavicle splints;
Restraints and dressing trays;
Batteries; tubing; all sorts of gloves;
Supplies to make your day!

Canes and crutches and underpads;
Anything the nurse would seek!
We've got it all! But—um—well,
It's backordered till next week!

IT RHYMES WITH "O"

Ten little Indians made of dough
Were standing neatly in a rough.
Then one fell over and hit my tough;
You should've heard me holler, "Ough!"

Then spoke up my loving bough,
"To the doctor, you should gough!"
To this I quickly answered, "Nough!
"It was just my little tough."

But it turned red and swollen, sough,
In good hot water, I soaked my tough.
Next time, I'll carefully make the rough
For ten little Indians made of dough!

THE HALLOWEEN PARTY

Through an old cemetery one Halloween,
While making my homeward track;
I heard a noise that sounded odd;
Like bones going "clickety-clack."
I turned aside to see the cause
Of this strange and eerie sound.
I saw a sight that left me cold
And froze me to the ground.

'Twas a Halloween party in full swing!
Like none I'd ever seen!
I could hardly believe my popping eyes!
I know my face turned green!
Up from the bottom of a shallow grave
Came the glow of an eerie light.
A tiny campfire, whose flickering sparks
Were piercing the chill, damp night.

A cauldron, black, sat in the flame
And bubbled its gruesome brew,
Stirred by a black-robed, cackling hag,
Who was making "Monster Stew."
Green-eyed cats, with coats of black,
Were gathered all around.

Watching goblins jump and dance;
Their laughter, a hideous sound.

The whitened bones of skeletons danced
And cast their shadows, black.
They dangled like puppets on a chain
And their bones went "clickety-clack."
My teeth were chattering; my heart went thump!
And I'd seen quite enough!
So, if my feet would take me home,
These critters could do their stuff!

I ran from there as fast as I could
And never once looked back!
I never again want to see or hear
Those bones going "clickety-clack!"

HALLOWEEN NIGHT

The fire was dying;
There was no light;
In my bed I was lying
    On Halloween night.

He came through the air,
A ghost in white,
To sit on my chair
    On Halloween night.

A witch on a broom
In the full moon's light,
Rode past my room
    On Halloween night.

Hobgoblins were playing;
Jack-o'-lanterns were bright;
The spooks were saying,
    "It's Halloween night!"

HALLOWEEN

Jack-o'-lanterns in the tree,
Smiling silly down at me.
Fiery mouth and nose and eyes
Looking anything but wise.

Cats and witches riding brooms,
Up they go; away they zoom.
I wish that I might fly so high,
But not with them! Oh no, not I!

Ghosts and goblins everywhere!
Oh, it does give me a scare!
Howling winds and moon so bright.
The world is spooky on Halloween night!

THE WITCHES' CAVE

High in the hills and deep in the earth
Is a cave no one has seen.
I'm told the witches gather there
On the eve of Halloween.

In the center of a shadowed room
A cauldron pot is stewing.
Who knows what odds and ends of things
The black-robed hags are brewing?

Green-eyed cats, as black as night,
Look out from shrouding gloom;
While witches cackle, wild with glee,
And pronounce their spells of doom.

Their brooms stand neatly in a row,
Geared for the midnight flight.
Soon, witches and cats will leave the cave
To ride by the full moon's light.

Who knows the way the witches will go,
Or the person they'll pursue?
I know this year at Halloween
I will not be out? Will you?

ME AND JOSHUA

Me and Joshua! Me and Joshua!
In a rocking chair; going nowhere!
Me and Joshua! Me and Joshua!
Who's the bestest of us all?
Me and Joshua!

I'M GOING HOME

Some of these days, when life is done,
I'm gonna hear Him say, "Well done."
'Twill be joy when I enter Heaven's door.
There'll be glory in that Land
Where there is no parting hand.
I'm gonna live with my Lord evermore.

I'm going home to be with Jesus.
I'm going home, no more to roam.
There to meet with friends and loved ones
Singing praises 'round the throne.
Some of these days, praise God, I'm going home.

I'll be free from all of Earth's fears
When I leave this vale of tears.
What a morning that will be when I reach home.
I will look on Jesus' face;
Praise Him for redeeming grace.
'Twill be glorious on that resurrection morn.

Sinner, come and join our band; go with us to that fair
        land.
We will leave behind all earthly toil and care.

We'll go sweeping thru the gates; oh, a blessed time
    awaits!

When we join in with that ransomed chorus there.

BECAUSE OF MY SINS

While life's blood came pouring down
From nails and a thorny crown,
    Alone on the tree
    Jesus died there for me.
That I might with Him be found.

Because of my sins, He died.
Because of my tears, He cried.
    Because of my care,
    A load, He did bear.
Because of my sins, He died.

Wicked within was I.
Sin-sick, condemned to die.
    With Him on the cross,
    Was nailed all my loss.
For me, Him they crucified.

BETHESDA'S POOL

For many long years, he had lain there in vain.
With no one to help him draw nigh,
Those beautiful waters, his healing to claim.
Then Jesus Himself passed by.

Oh, weary and footsore, the fountain is free;
Its waters refreshing and cool.
They're flowing and cleansing, and Jesus says, "Come.
"Enter Bethesda's pool."

"Wilt thou be whole?" asked the Master that day.
Come, enter the waters so cool.
Be cleansed and forgiven; oh, hear Jesus say,
"I am Bethesda's Pool."

LET THE BEAUTY OF THE LORD

Let the beauty of the Lord be on me!
Let the beauty of the Lord be on me!
　　May His glory and His grace
　　Be reflected in my face.
Let the beauty of the Lord be on me!

THIS SAME JESUS

This same Jesus! This same Jesus!
Rising to the clouds, oh, hear the angels say,
"He will come in like manner
"As you see Him go away."
This same Jesus will return for us someday!

About the Author

Linda Hughes has been writing poetry most of her adult life. She is an eighty-year-old widow, whose husband was an ordained minister and a pastor for nearly forty years. She still writes poetry, collects salt and pepper shakers, and plays the piano for the church she attends. She and her two daughters and their families live in Texas.

FAITH, FAMILY, AND FANTASY